It's

Great To

Pray

It's Great To Pray

KATHRYN WICKEY ORSO

Morehouse-Barlow Co. :: New York

Copyright © 1974
by Morehouse-Barlow Co., Inc.
14 East 41st Street
New York, New York 10017

ISBN: 0-8192-1177-X
Library of Congress Catalog Card No.: 74-80379

Printed in the United States of America

Preface

Through the past thirty years of my life, I have received complete and loving support from my dear husband, Paul. I wish to acknowledge the significant influence he has had upon my life as he encouraged my work and my witness and as he modeled God's love and acceptance.

Through all the years of my life, besides the influence of my parents, there have been authors, teachers, pastors, speakers, and friends who have given me insight into the nature of God and my relation to him in prayer. I recognize my indebtedness to those whose lives have touched mine in this way.

*To My Mother and Father
Ethel and Gould Wickey
My first teachers about God*

Contents

I
11 It's Great to be Able to Pray
II
18 It's Great to Pray to a Listening God
III
26 It's Great to Pray to an Accepting God
IV
34 It's Great to Pray to a Loving God
V
43 It's Great to Pray to a Forgiving God
VI
54 It's Great to Pray to a Powerful God
VII
61 It's Great to Pray to a Freeing God
VIII
70 It's Great to Pray to a Caring God
IX
79 It's Great to Pray to a Conquering God
X
86 It's Great to Pray for the Will of God

It's Great
To Be Able To Pray

It's Great To Be Able To Pray

I get so tired
  Of hearing that I ought
  To pray every day.
    I've heard it for years,
      Ever since I was a little girl,
    And that's a long, long time.
I ought to exercise every morning, too.
    And count calories,
    And keep the sink clear of dirty dishes,
    And not let my ironing pile up.

So I feel extremely guilty
  When I don't pray,
  And when I don't do
    All those other things, too.

Sometimes I still try,
Some days I really try
  Harder than others.

For one year, or maybe it was longer,
   I even prayed every day,
      Exactly at noon.
But I don't do it now—
   I haven't for some time.
      And, honestly, I seem to be managing.
         Quite well, I think.

It just seems that praying
   Often gets too mechanical for me.
      Every morning,
         If I remember.
      Every night,
         If I'm not too tired.
      Every meal,
         If I'm thankful or not.
Gradually it all becomes quite meaningless—
   So boring,
   So time–consuming,
   So uninteresting.

Maybe, I'm just not a person
   Who needs to pray regularly.
I do loving things every day.
   That's praying.
I admire beauty in nature.
   Isn't that praying?
I am grateful for all the good things in my life.
   Surely that's praying.

Still, there seems to be something missing.
   I just can't put my finger on it.
   I don't feel overwhelmingly loving,
      Most of the time.
   Nor am I a very lovely person,
      Some of the time.
   I am just not the person
      I'd really like to be.

Am I missing out on something?
   Where can I turn to find
      More meaning in life?
      More power?
      More beauty?
      More hope?
   Some of my friends seem to have it—
      Real peace,
      Inner beauty,
      Spiritual conviction.
         All qualities I want so badly
         For myself.

Could all these come from prayer?
   I wonder.

The thought keeps nagging at me,
   When I am upset and tired,
   When I am lonely and afraid,
   When I am mean and ugly.
      When I especially need a friend,
   I wonder.

Those who pray a lot
   Really believe in it.
It has changed many lives:
   St. Augustine found God himself,
   Martin Luther found power,
   John R. Mott found new vision,
   E. Stanley Jones found health.
Even Jesus needed prayer.

And there's Catherine Marshall,
         John Sutherland Bonnell,
         Norman Vincent Peale.
All these important people—
   They swear by prayer (if that's possible).
   They really believe in it.
      That's for sure.

Many songs have been written about prayer—
   Beautiful,
   Meaningful.

Lots of poetry can be found on prayer—
   Sentimental,
   Inspirational.
      Some published,
      Some not.

A multitude of books in the library are on prayer—
  Some good,
  Some not so good.
    A wide variety of titles
      On the psychology,
          the practice,
            the problems of prayer.
      And the wonder,
          the promise,
            the manner of prayer.
      And so many more.

You'd think
Prayer was the answer to everything.
  At least some people believe it so.
Many words have been written
  In one form or other
  On the subject of prayer.

I have sung many songs;
I have read many poems;
I have digested many books;
I have heard many sermons.
  And yet, I have not found meaning
    For my prayer life
    In any of these.
I wonder why?

Prayer must be experienced;
  It must be felt.

Maybe I should begin
  At the beginning.
And think

About my feelings,
About my thoughts,
About prayer.

What do I think about
  When I think about prayer?
    Praise to God,
    Thanksgiving for blessings,
    Confession of sin,
    Petition for forgiveness,
    Intercession for others.
These are included in prayer—
  Are important parts of prayer.

But how do I feel
  When I think about prayer?
    Duty and obligation?
      Perhaps.
    Joy and excitement?
      Maybe.
    Habit and routine?
      Sometimes.
    Fear and anxiety?
      Occasionally.
    Pleasure and power and privilege?
      Rarely.

Perhaps prayer is all of these
  Some of the time.
But most importantly
  Prayer is a privilege.
    An exciting privilege!

It's great to be able to pray!

It's Great To Pray To A Listening God

It's great to be able to pray!
Where else can I get so much for so little?
   A real bargain—
   Just what everybody wants.

Just imagine.
   A chance for communion with God,
   Talking with my heavenly father,
But more important,
   Listening to Him.

All I have to do is
   To be quiet for a little while.
      That's very hard for me.
      Is it hard for you, too?

There's so much hustle and bustle
   In my daily life:
      The clothes to be washed,
      The dishes in the sink,
      The children under foot.

It's hard to find a time
   When I can be alone with God,
   So I can talk uninterruptedly.
When no one is around:
   To pull on me,
   To ask why,
   To scream and holler,
   To cry and whine.
When I can listen to Him speak, too.
Without a lot of other voices around.
   Perhaps happy,
      or sad,
      or angry voices.
   But voices, nonetheless,
      Part of my world—
         An important part.
And sometimes they smother me
And shut out every other sound,
      Even God's voice.

God is the only one with whom I speak
   In prayer.
      He is the one I seek.
      He is the one I enjoy.

As I seek His nearness,
        His presence,
        His concern,
I am aware of His special love,
   Of a spiritual something,
      That I feel
      And experience.

God often speaks to me in prayer.
   In His loving presence,

    I find guidance and light.
  In His peace,
    I feel warmth and love.

Sometimes He speaks very quietly,
  And I have to listen very closely,
  Being quiet long enough
    To hear and understand Him.

Other times, He comes through
  Loud and clear.
  And the longer I talk with Him,
    the clearer I present my case,
    the more honest I am with Him,
      The sharper is the rebuke,
        If I need discipline;
      The brighter is the light,
        If I need guidance;
      The firmer is the support,
        If I need strength.

I can't hear God
  Unless I listen.
I can't listen to Him
  Unless I am in tune with Him,
  Unless I am in fellowship with Him—
    Expectantly,
    Eagerly,
      Awaiting His loving voice.

What's so special about fellowship with God?
  It's wonderfully special!

Just to be in God's presence
  And to be aware of it!

I know God is with me always,
   Though, sometimes,
   I'm not very conscious of it.

When I'm aware of His divine presence,
   I have inner strength,
        peace,
        serenity.

In the realization that God is with me
   My own problems seem lighter—
     The anger of my neighbor,
     The tears of my children,
     The exhaustion I feel.

I know that God will give me spiritual power
   To face my neighbor,
   To cope with my children,
   To understand myself.

Somehow I just don't get
   This radiant power
   From any other source—
     Not from my parents,
     Nor my friends,
     Nor my pastor,
     Not even from my husband,
   And they all love me, too.

Being with God is something so different.
For God is the best—
        the supreme—
           In love and goodness,
           In power and glory.

And fellowship with Him
   Is the highest privilege
      I can have.

In His presence
   My spirit is refreshed,
   A new life is offered me,
   My being is renewed,
   Greater strength is given me.

To raise my heart and mind to Him,
   I must love Him completely.
   I must trust Him absolutely—
      No half way measures,
      No ands or buts or ifs.

Then God can reach me.
   Through my love for Him,
   Through my trust in Him,
      I have confidence and freedom
         To accept His will,
         To follow His way.

I know, too, that God is love—
   Completely—
      Never sending me misery,
      Never giving me sorrow,
      Never inflicting pain on me.

God's true character is loving,
                       healing,
                         helping—
      Never hurting,
      Nor destroying.

This faith in God's love
Makes such a difference in my praying.
   I'm not afraid of God's wrath.
      He loves me.
   I don't fear His judgment.
      He loves me.
   I don't get angry with Him.
      He loves me.
   I don't have to plead with Him.
      He loves me.

It's wonderful to have a God
   Whose love is so tremendous.

I feel an inner peace
When I am with God—
   In the midst of sorrow or pain,
   In happiness or excitement.
It is truly the peace
   That passes understanding.

I am really overcome
With the wonder of it all.
   God is so holy,
        so powerful,
        so creative,
        so righteous.
   Yet, he is so forgiving
   And so loving
      When I am so lacking
      In these qualities myself.

I don't pray to win God's favor
Or to get His help.

I already have these,
Though I often forget.

But I do pray to harmonize my life with His
               to understand His will for me.

It's great to pray
To a listening God!

It's Great To Pray To An Accepting God

It's great to pray
To a God
　Who accepts me
　Just as I am.

Before God
　I can be just myself—
　With no pretenses.

I don't have to play games,
　When I just want to be myself.
I don't have to act nice,
　When I feel quite ugly.
I don't have to say kind words,
　When I'm thinking hateful thoughts.

God knows the way I really feel,
　　　　the thoughts I really think—
No matter how I act or
　　　　what I say to Him.

He loves me
Even when I'm not easy to love—
   When I don't look nice,
   When I'm not smiling,
   When I'm downright mean.

He understands me
Even when I don't understand myself—
   When I don't feel like
     combing my hair,
     trying to think positively,
     being a pleasant person.

It doesn't matter
What I think of myself.
   Some days I really have
   A mighty good opinion of me;
     Other days I don't think
     I'm worth anything at all.

Nor is God affected
By what others think I am.
   I'm sure I'm not
     As good as some people think.
   But then, neither am I
     As bad as others may say!

I don't have to spend any time
Convincing God of my true worth.
   He already knows.
     After all, He made me,
     And He loves me.

I'm sure He'd like it
   If I'd improve a little.

But his love isn't dependent
   On any promises of mine.

His love is complete,
   No matter what.

God knows me so well,
   I can't fool Him.
And I don't have to spend
   Any time trying.
I can start right where I am,
   With all my badness
   And with all my goodness, too.

God loves me,
   In spite of myself
   And because of myself.

The only way to come to God
   Is humbly and honestly.
It is the only way
   To expect God to hear me.
If I don't trust Him
Enough to be honest with Him,
   There's just no use praying.

Praying is a relationship
Between God and me—
   An open trust response
   Of me to God,
      Because I know Him,
      Because I trust Him.
He has come to me in love.
   I trust His love;
   So I pray.

It's important
   That I trust God enough
      To be honest
      To be myself
         Freely and frankly.

Moses and Job were free.
They didn't say
   What they thought God wanted to hear.
They were honest
   They said what they really thought.

Moses was critical of God;
   He even questioned God's actions.
Job complained that God
   Wasn't being fair to him.
Both men were honest with God.

Why is being honest so hard?
   Don't I want God
   To know me as I am—really?
      It's very necessary
         That I face the truth
            Maybe the awful truth,
            About myself.

God isn't impressed
With the masks I wear—
   The false pride,
   The smooth words,
   The charming manner.

God isn't convinced
With all my pretenses—

To be full of faith,
To be high in hope,
To be enthusiastic in service,
   When I'm really not.

Facing myself honestly
Is the first step
   To receiving God's power—
      Admitting I'm at a standstill,
         If I am.
      Admitting that I need help,
         If I do—
And the door is open
To God's strength.

Even though I have people around me,
   When I tell my God that I am lonely,
   He understands.

Even though I know about eternal life,
   When I tell my God that I am afraid of dying,
   He understands.

Even though I have family and friends,
   When I tell my God that I feel rejected,
   He understands.

I can talk over anything at all
With God,
   Even the unmentionables
   In my life.

God doesn't shrug off
My real concerns.

He believes me.
He comforts me,
   In pain,
   In sorrow,
   In fear.

God will have courage for me,
When I turn over to Him,
   My fears,
   My loneliness,
   My rejection.

My weakness won't stop God,
My fears don't frighten Him—
   He can deal with them.
   He can do all the courageous thinking
     For me,
       If I admit my problems,
       If I turn to Him,
   Instead of trying to wrestle with them,
     All alone.

God will find a way to work through me
And through my problems.

God can work
With just a little faith,
       a little trust.
   Remember the widow's pennies,
       the small boy's lunch,
       the tiny mustard seed,
       the bit of yeast.

His power is great
When I give it a chance.

How great God is.
How wonderfully great
  That I can pray to a God
  Who accepts me
    With no strings attached.

It's great to pray
To an accepting God.

It's Great
To Pray To A Loving God

God loves me personally,
Just think of that!
   Above all the splendor in the world,
   Above all the wonders of the earth,
     He loves me.

God takes an interest in me.
He cares about me.
   Even as He counts the hairs on my head,
   Even as He cares when a sparrow falls,
   Even as He knows each star in the heaven,
     He is concerned about me.

Even though there are millions more to love,
God loves me.
   As though there were no one else to love,
   God loves me.

God can do the impossible—
   He can love
   Each one of many.
      Individuals do make up multitudes.
      And God loves each one.
He knows us all
By name.

There's no way
God can love the world,
   Without loving
   Each person in it.

Isn't it great!
God loves me
   As one among many,
   And, yet, as a very special one.

God loves me
Completely.
   And wills only that which
   Brings me real happiness.

If my own foolishness
And wrong choices
   Keep me from true joy,
God will give me
Another chance in eternity.
   He loves me that much.

God in His mercy
Wants to save me
   From my sin

From my wrong doing.

God created me.
  In His great love
  He gave me life—
    My wonderful body
      With all its intricate functions,
    My growing mind
      With its ability to understand.

His love is revealed
Through my uniqueness
  My own special qualities
    That make me, ME.
      He made me different from you
      And you different, too,
        From everyone else.
        No carbon copies!

God surrounded me
With beauty.
  And gave me the sensitivity
  To enjoy it—
    The sunrise and sunset,
    The stars and moon,
    The flowers and trees,
      And so much more.
All revealing more of God's love.

It's great to pray to a God
Who shows His love
  In and through and above
  Everything that happens.

Through all else—
Through His power,
   His judgment,
   His forgiveness,
   His creativity,
Stands His love.

The way I pray
Is affected by
 What I think of God,
 How I think God acts,
 Who I think God is.

To Amos and Isaiah,
 God was a righteous being
 Without pity.
They were prophets of doom.

To Jesus,
 God was a loving person
 With compassion and concern.
Jesus cried over Jerusalem.

I know God's love compensates,
 For all my suffering and loss.
I know His love is working,
 Through all the impersonal laws of nature.
I know He loves each of us,
 Whoever we are,
 Wherever we are,
  No matter what happens to us
  As a result of our sin,
   Or of someone else's sin.

God does not send illness
   To punish us.
He does not permit tragedy
   To educate us.
He does not inflict suffering
   To test us.

My God loves us so much—
   When we cry or suffer or hurt,
   He cries and suffers and hurts.

God by His very loving nature
   Couldn't create a deformed baby,
   Couldn't give cancer to anyone,
   Couldn't cause a hurricane to wreck havoc.

In His love
God wills that
   All children have perfect bodies,
   All people have good health,
   No one be destroyed by natural law.

Our love for a friend is small
Compared with God's love
   For him.
Our concern for his health is nothing
Compared with God's wish
   For his health.
He loves him—and me—
   Completely.

It is impossible for me
Ever to understand completely

God's love.
    It is so great,
    It is so all-encompassing,
    Beyond my comprehension.

I just need
To accept God's love
  In faith.

After all,
God sent Jesus
  To show me His love,
  To prove to me He cares.
    And what a price He paid!
"Jesus loves me, this I know,
For the Bible tells me so."
    What greater revelation!

Jesus revealed
God's faith in me—
  Permitting me to be free,
    Not to love,
    Not to serve,
    Not to forgive.
But God's hope is
    That I will love,
    That I will serve,
    That I will forgive.

In His love
He has shown me the way,
  Through His son,
  Through the lives of others,
  Through my own experiences with Him.

God loves me.
He sent His Holy Spirit
   To be a constant reminder that
      as I work,
      as I play,
      as I pray,
I am surrounded by God's love,
By the Spirit of a loving God.

As a child of God
I was made in His likeness—
   For goodness and truth,
   For beauty and love,
   For God.

As a good Father,
God loves and cares for me...
   He is concerned about me—personally.

He will give me
His guidance and direction,
His support and comfort.
   He will not leave me alone
   To wander and to drift.

In God's great love,
He has a good purpose
   For my life.

God loves.
God *is* love—
   Not abstract,
   Nor aloof,
   Nor preoccupied,

But present,
And sharing,
And revealing.

All that I know about God
Is through His love,
   Through His creation,
   Through His revelation.

God's love,
God's loving,
   All surround me,
     In what He does for me,
     In what He does through me,
       In what he does for others,
       In what He does through others,
Through His continuing creation,
Through His ongoing revelation.

It's great to pray
To a loving God!

IT'S GREAT
TO PRAY TO A FORGIVING GOD

It's Great To Pray To A Forgiving God

It's great to pray
To a forgiving God.
  In His great love,
  God forgives me.
    Without criticizing me,
    Without scolding me,
    Without judging me,
      With lots of loving,
      God forgives.

My secret thoughts—
  Sometimes evil—
    Don't shock Him.
My bitterness—
  Sometimes uncalled for—
    Doesn't upset Him.
My many shortcomings—
  Sometimes downright sinful—
    Don't make God think less of me.

I really do think
   Some pretty bad thoughts sometimes.
   And God forgives me,
      When I tell Him about them.

I often fail
   To do loving things
   And God forgives me,
      When I say I'm sorry.

I feel very guilty
   About things I say—
      Judging and criticizing—
   And God forgives me,
      When I confess my guilt.

God forgives me—period.
   He doesn't make a big issue
   Out of my failures.
      He accepts my badness
      As part of me.
   And forgives,
   And forgives,
   And forgives.
He forgives me
Without any harsh judgment.

God is ready to forgive
Even when I am not ready to ask.
   He knows I am in trouble
      Even though I don't.

Jesus gave forgiveness
Even when it wasn't sought:

"Forgive them
   For they know not
   What they do."

For my growth and development,
I need to confess to God
   My wrongs,
   My lies,
   My thoughts.
      To help me understand
      When I need help,
         When I have done wrong.

I need to talk with God
   About my needs and desires,
   About my failures and successes,
To receive the assurance of forgiveness
   When I am all mixed up
   And not doing God's will.

I need daily forgiveness,
   So my guilt doesn't pile up,
   So my sins don't get the better of me.

Nothing is too simple.
Nothing is too complex—
   Too bad,
   Too evil,
To talk over with God.

God has lots of time—
   Eternity.
      He'll listen patiently.
      He'll forgive eternally.

Forgiveness is mine
  For the asking
  And asking,
  And asking.

If I really want
To be forgiven—
  And I do,
  Or I wouldn't ask—
    I will try to be better.
    I won't keep on sinning.

I don't ask forgiveness
For that which I intend
  To keep on doing.
    That wouldn't make sense.

Receiving forgiveness
Doesn't build a wall
  Around me,
    Protecting me from more sin,
    Protecting me from future temptation.

The assurance of forgiveness
Does give me strength
  To see my sin
    More clearly,
  To deal with my sin
    More honestly,
  To face my sin
    More courageously.

God's promise of forgiveness
Gives me the strength

To forgive myself,
To forgive others.

I must learn
To forgive the little things
  That annoy me,
    And make me mad—
      Promises not kept,
      White lies told,
      Talk behind my back,
It's sometimes hard to forgive,
Much harder than it should be.

I must learn
To forgive the big things
  That seem inexcusable,
  Surely unforgiveable—
    Uncontrolled temper,
    Breaking the law,
    Using profanity.

Small or large sins,
All sins against me,
  To a greater
  Or less degree.
    I have it in my power
      To needle and remind,
      To scream and blast,
        Or to forgive and forget,
        And to love and accept,
          To the best of my ability.

My ego
Is part of the problem—

I get hurt,
I feel "put down."
My pride
Is affected—
   I lash out,
   I blow up.
      The problem is multiplied—
      I feel worse, not better.

It's much easier,
And more human,
   To get angry,
   And not to love,
   To, at least, hold a grudge.

It becomes easier
And more divine-like,
   When God helps me,
   When God forgives me,
      For me to forgive
      For me to love.

"Forgive me as I forgive."
   I must give forgiveness,
   If I hope to receive forgiveness.
      God makes it clear.
      I find it so hard.

I must forgive
   As much as I really can,
      To obey His command,
      To obtain His forgiveness.

Forgiving,

As God forgives,
  Means forgetting.
    No conditions,
    No "if you don't, I will,"
    No "if you do, I won't,"
    No resentment,
    No grudges.

It is hard
For me to forgive myself
  Much less to forgive others.

I expect
  To pay a price,
  To be punished,
When I have done wrong.

And sometimes I feel better
  When I have suffered,
  When I have hurt,
For what I have done.

Yet, the more guilt I feel,
The more self-condemnation,
  The more worthless I become,
  The less worthy I feel.

Maybe that's the problem
Right here.
  I have trouble forgiving myself.
  And unless I forgive myself,
    I do not have a forgiving spirit
    To forgive anyone else.

The more aware I am
Of my own guilt,
    The more forgiving I should be
    Of the sins of others.

There's a relationship
    Between my forgiving myself
    And my forgiving others;
        Between my acceptance of myself
        And my acceptance of others.

Both are related
To my understanding
    Of God's forgiveness,
    Of God's acceptance,
        Of me,
        Of others.

Forgive me as I forgive.
Really?
    Who am I to withhold forgiveness?
    Only God who is perfect
        Can withhold forgiveness.
"He who is without sin."

I have no choice.
    To do God's will,
    To obey His command,
I must forgive.

Forgiving means loving.
Forgiving means accepting—
    No matter what is done to me,

No matter what is said about me,
   Or about my loved ones.

God does require a lot of me,
   I, who am so very human.

There can't be
   As much forgiveness on my part
   As there is on God's;
I'm just too human.

God in His love,
   Knowing my weakness,
   Expects me at least to try
     To forgive others.

In my trying to forgive,
My reconciling attitude to others,
   God hears my confession
     Of my own unkindness,
     Of my own anger,
     Of my own self-righteousness.

He hears my admission of complacency,
        my admission of indifference,
        my admission of lack of vision.
And God forgives me.

I leave my sins
With God.
   The sins of which I am aware,
    The sins of which I'm not aware,
     Knowing He'll understand,
     Knowing He'll forgive.

I am aware
That unless I am careful
  I'll fall again,
  I'll make mistakes again,
  I just won't do some things
    That I really ought to do.

And God will continue to forgive.

It's great to pray
To a forgiving God!

IT'S GREAT
TO PRAY TO A POWERFUL GOD

It's Great To Pray To A Powerful God

It's great to pray
 to a God with power.
It's great to share
 in the power of God.

Fortunately,
 God can work without me.
Wouldn't it be tragic
If His kingdom depended on me?
 On my succeeding,
  When I fail so often?
 On my rising,
  When I fall so frequently?
 On my solving problems,
  When I really don't know how?

Just think
Of the overwhelming responsibility
  If Christ had only me
    To serve Him in the world
      This day!

It's wonderful to know
  That God does not really need me,
  But He does really love me.
    That God is independent of me,
    But I am dependent on Him.

If I fail or fall
Or don't know how,
  God will find others.
The whole future of God
  Doesn't depend on me.

The world is in
God's good, strong hands,
  Not mine.
    What a blessed relief!

But how great it is
To share in God's work,
  If I choose!
What a joy to share
In His power,
  If I am able!

The more I turn to God,
The better I know His will,
The keener I am
  In understanding His mind.

My life becomes so open to God,
  That all my thoughts,
  That all my actions,
Are, in fact, a constant prayer.

My praying is not
An attempt to change God's mind.
  But an attempt to find out
  What is God's mind.
Not an effort to bring Him around
To my way of thinking,
  But to tune in
  To His way of thinking.
Not a plea
To overcome God's reluctance,
  But an effort
  To determine what is His holy will.
Not a drive to persuade God
To do something against His nature,
  But to harmonize my nature,
  With His divine nature.
    Allowing God to permeate me—
      That's what prayer is all about.
    Wanting God to clean me up,
      To make my desires
      More acceptable to Him.

Naturally,
I'm not looking for trouble,
  But when it hits
  I want God with me.
    I want His strength
    To be my strength.

In prayer,
I do not beg or coax God.
   He's not reluctant or stubborn.

In prayer,
I don't tell or inform God.
   He's not ignorant or ill-informed.

In prayer,
I do not plead with God.
   He's not unfeeling or uncaring.

It is I
   Who am reluctant,
     and ignorant,
     and insensitive.

God wants
So much more for me
   Than I ever think
   To ask Him to give me.

I pray for peace
   And I know that God wants peace, too,
   And gives me the energy
     To work for peace.
     I am God's channel.

I pray for my cancer-ridden friend
   And I know that God loves her, too,
   And he gives me insights
     To help her creatively.
     I surrender my will to His.

Surrender!
There's the key.
   Yielding my will,
   All of it.

"Not my will,
 But Thine be done."
So easily said.
But so deep
   In ultimate meaning.

Yielding my purpose,
Yielding my life,
   To God,
   To be used by Him.

God works through me,
To help bring about a creative change—
   In my own life,
   In the life of a friend,
   In the life of the world.

In prayer,
I find divine help—
   To experience more of God's love,
   To make God's love visible to others.

God can change others,
   As He helps me change,
   As He shows me love.

My world gets better
When I ask God to change me

More than wanting Him
To change others.
When I pray for my own forgiveness
More than for the sins
Of others.

It makes a difference
In my praying
Where I put the need for change
and the need for help,
On me—not always—on others.

Through prayer,
I share in God's creativeness.
He gives me power
Much greater than my own.

Through prayer,
I share in God's power,
In God's creative power.

It's great to pray
To a powerful God!

It's Great
To Pray To A Freeing God

It's Great To Pray To A Freeing God

God's power
Is reflected
  In my freedom.
    Only an omnipotent God
    Could take the chance
      Of giving me or you
      Free will.

God has power
To achieve His purpose
  Ultimately,
    In spite of my sin,
    In spite of my stubbornness.
      He gives me freedom to choose.

God's great power
Is revealed
  In His ability
  To win His goal
    And not to deny my freedom
    In the process.

God gives me free reign
   To choose His way, or—
  To reject His will.

If God suppressed my will,
If God denied my choice,
   He would admit defeat,
   He would show weakness.

Nothing can defeat
God's power—
  Ultimately.
     Not even man's freedom.

God is in His heaven,
His power will reign,
   No matter how I or others
     Block His will...
     Mix things up.

Part of God's creation in me
Is the ability to choose—
   My power to make decisions,
   My freedom to act.

In God's great love,
He gives me a share
   In creating in His image,
    In determining certain events.
     To some extent,
     He lets me choose
       The direction of my life,
       The development of my abilities.

God gives me freedom.
And each day
  He restores this freedom,
    Which I often misuse,
      In ignorance, and—sometimes—
    Quite willfully.

It seems to me
God takes a lot of risk
  When He permits me freedom.
    Not dominion,
    Not a single puppet string,
      But complete freedom,
      Which He himself never violates.

When He could have kept
Complete control so easily,
  He chose instead
  To give me freedom.

God cares
What I do with this freedom,
  But He doesn't force
  His will on me—
    Nor on anyone else.

It's wonderful
To be free,
  To choose what I will do,
  To choose what I won't do.

Some people
Call it "surrender."
  Relinquishing my will,

But only if I choose;
   Keeping my will
   If I choose instead.

I'm free to keep my will
And I'm free to follow His.
   It's all up to me.
   What an awesome responsibility!

Surrender?
Relinquish?
Give up?
   What do I surrender?
   What do I give up—
     When I pray, really pray?

I must be willing
   To relinquish,
   To give up
     My hateful attitudes,
     My nasty temper,
     My sinful desires.

I don't surrender,
I don't part with
   My integrity,
   My personhood.

My being is enhanced,
My self is strengthened,
   As I let God pervade my inner life,
   As I get rid of the sinful me.

I must give up my sinfulness

Voluntarily,
Freely,
   If I give it up at all.
It must be my choice.
The responsibility is mine.

I'm free, free, free,
   To make real choices,
   To be responsible
      For my decisions.

Certainly I'm bound
   By definite personal limitations—
      The conditions of my body,
      The limits of my mentality,
      The extent of my education.
   By the society in which I was born—
      Its laws,
      Its cultural forces,
      Its stage of development.

But I can think
What I want to—
   Positive or negative thoughts,
   Happy or hateful thoughts,
      In every situation.

I can do what I want to—
   Right or wrong,
   Good or bad,
      In most situations.

In many ways,
I'm dependent upon God.

I can't live without His power
  In my body,
  In my mind,
  In the world.

In a flash,
  My heart could stop beating,
  My mental processes could fail,
  The earth could blow up.

Yet God frees me—
  To use my physical abilities
    Or to lie around the house,
  To develop my mental talents
    Or to let them be stagnant,
  To share my social gifts
    Or to lock myself in the kitchen.

He doesn't make me
Do what I don't want to do.
  He makes it possible for me
  To do just about anything
  I set my mind to do—
    To be deaf, dumb, and blind, or
    To hear, speak, and see.

God doesn't force me
Against my will.
  He doesn't whip me into shape
  Until I do His will,
    If I want to or not.

He frees me
  To be dynamic,

To be energetic,
To be creative.

I can be all these things
So much better because it's part of
  My God-given potential,
    Because God loves me,
    Because God guides me.

In my freedom,
  I can defeat the will of God,
    At least for a period of time.
  I can do what I want to do
    In harmony with God's will,
    Or contrary to it.
      That's my free choice.

Every situation
Is not God's will.
  But I'm free to find God's will
    In every situation.

All that happens
Is not of God's doing.
  But I'm free to find
  What God would have me do
    In all that happens.

I'm free to find God's will,
Then free to do it.
  Without this freedom
  Prayer would be
    Quite meaningless,
    Without purpose.

Freedom to pray,
Freedom not to pray,
   To cooperate or
   Not to cooperate,
That's what it's all about.

In my freedom,
   If I try to find God's will,
      He will guide me.
   If I seek to do His will,
      He will help me.
   If I follow His will,
      God will be with me.

God takes responsibility
For what happens,
   If I do His will.
      The results of His will
      Are His responsibility,
         Not mine.

My oneness with God
My at-one-ment
   Comes through my own decision,
   Comes by the grace of God.

God gives me the choice
And the freedom
   To accept His love
   Which he so freely gives.

It's great to pray
To a freeing God.

It's Great
To Pray To A Caring God

It's Great To Pray To A Caring God

God cares for me.
God cares for other people, too.
   As God loves me,
   So God loves others, too.

So I pray for those
   About whom I am concerned,
   For whom I care.

Of course, I must
Pray for other folks.
   I see their heartaches,
      their sickness,
      their sin,
   And I talk it over with God.
   I see their happiness,
      their joy,
      their success,
   And I thank God for these.

They and I have a bond
Which becomes stronger
  In prayer,
    Because I care,
    Because I know God cares.

It's so natural
To talk with God
  About folks
  Both of us love.

It's really inevitable.
As in my conversation
  With friends,
  With neighbors,
    We talk about folks,
      We know,
      We care about.

So in my prayer
With God
  I share my thoughts
  About those whom He and I know
    And care about.

I wonder
  If my prayers for someone else
  Make a difference to God?
    Or does it matter
    Only to me?

I believe
  God does hear,
  God does care,

When I pray for others.

When I pray
For others,
  God's spirit comes to them
    Releasing spiritual energy,
    Imparting powerful healing.

I can't prove it,
I can't explain it,
  I just believe it.

God is real.
His power transcends
  All natural barriers.

When I pray for others
I can resolve
  To be more kind,
  To be more thoughtful.
    (I can make resolutions
    Without praying, however!)

But if my prayer
Did even that—
  Just move me
  In the right direction—
    It would have
    Lots of value.

I can't pray for my enemy
And not want to forgive.
  I can't pray for my friend
  And not want to help.

Praying for those I love
Isn't putting the whole responsibility
   On God,
      For their actions and attitudes,
      For their health and well-being.

Praying does stimulate me
   To wiser acceptance
   Of my own responsibility
      For others.

As I talk it over with God
   I see the situation more clearly,
   I understand problems more rationally.
      God gives me light.

But I must be careful, so very careful,
   Not to manipulate,
   Not to force my will on others,
      In my prayers.

There's such a difference
   Between my caring
      And my possessing,
   My freeing
      And my owning.

Only as I learn the difference,
   Can I be free enough,
   Can I be loving enough,
      Really to help others.

Only as I learn
To let others be free, too,

    Can I open doors to God
    That they may enter.

The problem is
    My wanting others to be different—
        My friends to change their attitudes,
        My neighbors to be more considerate,
        My parents to be more patient.

My prayers
   About my friends,
   About my neighbors,
   About my parents,
Are my judgments about them.

My prayers
Often set me up as the judge,
   The one who really knows
      How others should think,
      How they should act,
      How they should be.

Please, God,
    Help my friends be more kind,
    Make my neighbors more thoughtful,
    Give my parents extra grace.

And when these prayers
Don't seem to change
   The people involved,
   I wonder why.

I may be making
The lives of others,

Their attitudes,
Their actions,
   Too much the focus
   Of my prayers.

Am I their keeper?
My prayers sound like it.
   Am I their judge,
     And sometimes jury, too?
       It often seems so
       When I am praying.

I have the answers
To what others should be,
   And, often,
     What they should not be.

Maybe I'm praying
Too much for others,
   That they be different.

Maybe I'm overly possessive,
Too presumptive,
   Of others' needs and concerns.

Am I really showing
Love and care
   For others?
Or am I revealing
Weaknesses and problems
   Of my own?

It's not my responsibility
To make the blueprint

For the lives of others.
   God takes care of that.

It's not my job
To tell God what to do
   For my friends and family.
     God knows
What is best for them.

God, let me pray
That I can be the channel
   Through whom You can work.

Let me release
My friends and loved ones
   From my possessiveness,
   From my knowing what is best.
     Help me give them over to You.

It's mighty hard,
For it often seems
   That I do know
   What is best
     For almost everyone.

But I don't have
To be the judge.
   I can accept everyone
   Just as they are,
     As God accepts me—
       Without reservation,
       Without qualification,
       Without judgment.

And then pray for others,
In a complete
   And accepting way.

It's so easy to criticize
When I really don't know
   The condition of someone's spiritual life
   Or their relationship to God.
     Outward appearances
     Aren't always accurate.

It's so hard
To keep me
   Out of my prayers
   For the others in my life.

God will help me,
As I ask for His guidance,
   To respect the integrity of others,
   To give them freedom to be themselves
     And not the persons
     I think they should be.

It's great to pray
To a God whose love
   Permeates all of life,
To a God who knows (better than I do)
   What is best for me,
   What is best for others, too.

It's great to pray
To a caring God.

It's Great
To Pray To A Conquering God

It's Great
To Pray To A Conquering God

It's hard to understand
Why there is suffering,
       and sickness,
       and disaster.

It's hard to understand
Why God permits
  These evils to exist.

With all His power
He could wipe out
  All evil,
  All trouble,
    If He chose.
      I'm sure He could.

But for some reason
God has limited Himself

By giving me freedom
   To do as I please,
By His own decision
   To create an orderly world.

God sees my troubles
From a different point of view.
   As bad as it is right now,
   As much as I really hurt today,
     One hundred years from now—
     Or in eternity—
       My pain won't matter.
       My unhappiness won't count.

God's love will be supreme.
My faith will be answered.

God knows what is best
In the total situation.
   His perspective is all-inclusive—
     Not just for today,
     But for yesterday,
     And for tomorrow, also.

As a good Father,
He does what is best—
   Because of my prayers,
   In spite of my prayers.

As a good child,
I trust my loving God;
   I share my heartfelt desires,
   I share my innermost needs
     When I talk with Him.

God never promised
I would not have suffering,
   Or pain,
   Or hardship.

God did promise
I would have His love,
   His care,
   His guidance.

No one is spared
The suffering
   That is part of being human,
   That is part of being in this world.

I do have certain resources,
Not used by everyone,
   Confidence in God's love,
   Faith in God's promises.

Evil itself
Does not make men strong.
   Often, it destroys.
     It is not in itself
     Creative of good.

But from evil can come
   That which is better.

God does not need
  To allow suffering
  To give me courage,
    But from suffering
    Often comes courage.

God does not need
   To allow hardship,
   To make me strong,
      But from hardship
      Often comes strength.

Trial and tribulation
   Are not essential
   To spiritual growth,
      But growth can come
      From trial and tribulation.

I can,
With God's help,
   Learn courage through danger,
   Know joy through selfless love,
   Share responsibility through living.
      The good and the bad,
      The sufferings and the sins,
         Of one of us
         Affects all of us.

My praying,
My faith,
My courage,
   All make a difference
   In the way I accept
      The evil in my life.

Good can come from evil,
Strength can come from weakness,
Courage can come from fear,
   If I let God guide me,
   If I use His wisdom in my life.

In God's great love,
Evil will not have
  The final word.
My suffering and hardship
Will not determine,
  One way or the other,
  My admission to heaven.

God will have
The last word
  In eternity;
God's love,
God's righteousness,
  Will reign eternally.

No evil,
No suffering,
No tragedy,
  In the last analysis,
  Can defeat God
    And His loving will.

I do know
  God loves me and you.
  God cares for me and for you.

Through our suffering
God wants us to have courage,
  And faith,
  And trust,
    In His love.

Some day,
  God will answer

My troubled questions;
  God will tell me
My faith is answered;
  God will show me the reason
  He allowed so much to happen
  Not according to His will.

There's just no way
God would allow
  Anything to happen
  That would defeat His holy will,
  Ultimately.

It's great to pray
To a God
  Who can overcome
  Evil with good.

It's great to pray
To a God
  Who will conquer
  All that is evil—
    If not in this world
    Then, in the next world.

IT'S GREAT
TO PRAY FOR THE WILL OF GOD

It's Great To Pray For The Will Of God

God's will—
What is God's will?
   I wonder.

I really want
God to will
   All that is pleasant,
   All that is comfortable,
     For me and those I love.
   No pain,
   No struggle,
   No hardship,
     Please!

When things happen
That do hurt or harm,
   I wonder.
     Were they God's will?
     Really God's will?

It rains "on the just and the unjust"
  That's the way it is...
    My being a good person
    Doesn't mean the weather
      Will suit me,
      Will be sunny and bright,
        Where I am.
          (Although the prayers of some
          Seem to ask just that.)

When our daughter was married,
I prayed for a sunny day.
  When a hurricane was approaching,
  I prayed it would blow out to sea.
    When we had just planted grass seed,
    I prayed for a light spring shower.

Were my prayers in vain
  In this world of established law?
  In this world of predictable results?

Just to suit my own desires
Am I asking God to change
  His natural order?

I guess I really am.
And yet, I've got to be honest
  With my God
  Who loves me.

To pray at all,
I must let God know
  My deep desires,
  My real hopes.

Talking it over with God
   Helps my wishes
   Get in proper perspective,
      Subjects my purposes
      To God's will,
         Gets me on God's wave length,
         Part of the joy of prayer.

Wouldn't it be a calamity
If, somehow, each of us
   Could control the weather,
   Just to suit our desires?

God was so wise
To set in motion
   A natural order
   For the universe.

But why does
The order of things
   Include so much that is harmful
   And so much that is disastrous?

God is not helpless
In the world He created.
   God is not limited
   By the laws He established.
      God is not confined
      To the level of understanding
         That I have.

When I don't understand
   About the tornadoes,
   About the hurricanes,

About the floods,
I figure
God will make it clear
  Some day.

Since these are events
I cannot change
  I'll do my best
  To see God's love,
    To be God's channel,
   In and through
  All that is unchangeable,
  All that is unpleasant
    Around me.

I wonder about
All the sickness and disease
  In the world about me.
    Are they part
    Of the will of God?

My friend's child became sick,
And she called the doctor.
  Was she fighting the will of God?
    And she gave him medicine,
    And she took him to the hospital.
  Was she resisting God's will?
    When he died,
    Her friends said,
      "It was God's will;
      Find His peace."

Surely God willed

That her child should live.
  God wills health and happiness
  For all His children.
    But he died.
    He had a disease,
      Man could not cure.

God willed
That my friend
  Find peace in the knowledge
    Of God's love,
  Find courage to help
    Fight disease,
  Find strength to comfort
    Others in their grief,
      When hers had healed.

God can use
Even sickness and health
  To make me strong,
  To give me faith.

Another friend
Had a fatal disease.
  She knew it.
  I knew it.
But her spiritual health,
  Her faith, hope, and love,
  Were a blessing to all.
    Her physical sickness
    Was not God's will.
Her spiritual health
Was God's will.

She may not have had
The same spiritual awareness
　　If she had been
　　Physically strong.
　　　　Only God knows.

Why does God allow
All this to happen,
　　If it is not His will?
It's so hard to understand.
　　God allows
　　What He does not want
　　　　To happen
　　　　To you and me.

Of course,
You and I bring about
　　Much of the pain,
　　Much of the sorrow,
In the world today.

The murder in war,
The illnesses about us,
The floods and droughts,
　　Coming from human weakness,
　　Coming from overindulgences,
　　Coming from careless destruction,
　　　　All cause much misery.

I can't blame God
For that which I
　　And people like me
Bring about ourselves
　　Upon each other.

"The will of God"
  Hardly.
      The result of sin,
      Obviously.

I bring much pain on myself,
   By fear,
   By guilt,
   By hate,
   By self-pity.

Psychologists and psychiatrists,
Ministers and educators all say
   My own perception
   Is important,
      To my outlook,
      To my mental health,
      To my physical strength, too.

I can make myself sick
Yes, really feel pain,
   When I am tense with worry,
   When I am rigid with fear,
   When I am filled with distrust.

This isn't God's fault,
It isn't His will,
   It's all my own doing,
   And my undoing, too.

Evil is in the world,
There's no doubt about it.
   But it isn't from God's hand.

Yet I blame Him.
It makes my suffering
  Easier to bear.
    When I can say,
    "It was the will of God,"
      I grow in resignation,
        Instead of growing in courage;
      I grow in martyrdom,
        Instead of growing in
          Spiritual health.

It negates
My personal responsibility,
  When I say,
  "It was the will of God."
I don't have
To change myself
  Or work for change about me,
    When I attribute evil,
    When I blame sickness,
    When I credit death,
      To the will of God.

I sit back
And get much comfort
  As I say that the tragedies
    And the evil
      In your life and
      In my life
  Are surely God's will.

If I really faced
The mistakes and the sin,

Which cause much of the trouble
   In the world,
My reactions would be
Quite different.

It is God's will
That I be strong and courageous,
That I grow in all spiritual ways,
   As a response to His love
   In gratitude for His love.

I must be careful
When I say,
   "It is the will of God."
     I may just be wrong.
       I may be speaking selfishly;
       I may be avoiding responsibility;
       I may be judging others.

What then is left?
   I must rely on faith
     That God listens and accepts,
     That God loves and forgives,
     That God cares and frees.
   I must trust that God wills
     Health and happiness,
     Life and love,
     Peace and progress.

With this faith,
   I pray and God listens.
     Then God speaks,
     And I understand.

This book has been composed in 11-point Fairfield at Trade Composition Service, Inc., in Walden, New York.

Printing and binding were done at Worzalla Publishing Company, Stevens Point, Wisconsin.